Key To Health

Mahatma Gandhi

rajpal

1912-2012
100
Years of Excellence in Publishing

rajpal

₹ 80

ISBN : 978-93-5064-101-9

Edition : 2013

© Rajpal & Sons

KEY TO HEALTH

by Mahatma Gandhi

Printed : Deepika Enterprises, Delhi

RAJPAL & SONS
Kashmere Gate, Delhi-110 006
Phone : 011-23869812, 23865483, Fax : 011-23867791
website : www.rajpalpublishing.com
e-mail : sales@rajpalpublishing.com

Publisher's Note

This book combines the two books on health which Mahatma Gandhi wrote in his lifetime "Key to Health" and "The Moral Basis of Vegetarianism". In these books Mahatma Gandhi spelt out his philosophy on how to maintain good health. Some ideas were included in both the books; the common text which appeared in both the books has been retained at only one point, so that the reader is not burdened with repetitive matter.

CONTENTS

SECTION I : Key to Health

1. The Human Body — 11
2. Air — 14
3. Water — 16
4. Food — 18
5. Condiments — 27
6. Tea, Coffee and Cocoa — 29
7. Intoxicants — 31
8. Opium — 34
9. Tobacco — 36
10. Brahmacharya — 39

SECTION II : Natural Therapeutics

11. Earth — 49
12. Hydrotherapy — 53
13. Ether *(Akash)* — 59
14. Sun — 63
15. Importance of Air — 65

SECTION III : The Moral Basis of Vegetarianism

16.	Food Values	69
17.	Unfired Food	70
18.	Vegetarianism	73
19.	Not An End In Itself	76
20.	The Moral Basis of Vegetarianism	78
21.	Our Daily Diet	83
22.	Minimum Diet	87

SECTION I

Key to Health

❀ ❀ ❀

Man becomes what he eats.
The grosser the food, the grosser the body

1

THE HUMAN BODY

It is necessary to understand the meaning of the word health, before entering upon a description of the human body. He is a healthy man whose body is free from all diseases; he carries on his normal activities without fatigue. Such a man should be able with ease to walk ten to twelve miles a day, and perform ordinary physical labour without getting tired. He can digest ordinary simple food. His mind and his senses are in a state of harmony and poise. This definition does not include prize fighters and such like. A man with extraordinary physical strength is not necessarily healthy. He has merely developed his musculature, possibly at the expense of something else.

> *A man with extraordinary physical strength is not necessarily healthy*

It is necessary to have enough knowledge of the human body which is expected to attain the above standard of health.

God alone knows what kind of education was prevalent in ancient times. Research workers on the subject may be able to tell us something, but only something, about it. But all of us have some experience of modern education in this country. It has no relation with our everyday life. Thus, it leaves us almost utterly ignorant about our own body. Our knowledge of our own village and our fields shares a similar fate. We are taught on the other hand, much about things which have no bearing on our daily life. I do not mean to say that such knowledge is of no use. But every thing has its own place. We must first know enough of our own body, our own house, our village and its surroundings, the crop that grows there and its history before going on to anything else. General knowledge broad-based on this primary knowledge, alone can enrich our life.

The human body is composed of what the ancient philosophers have described as the five elements. These are earth, water, vacancy, light and air.

All human activity is carried on by means of the mind aided by the ten senses. These are the five senses of action, i.e. hands, feet, mouth, anus and the genitals, and the five senses of perception, i.e. the nose, of taste through the tongue, of seeing through the eyes and of hearing through the ears. Thinking is the function of the mind and some people have called the eleventh sense. In health all the senses and the mind act in perfect co-ordination.

The inner working of the human machine is wonderful. The human body is the universe in miniature. That which cannot be found in the body is not found in the universe. Hence the philosopher's formula, that the universe within reflects the universe without. It follows therefore that our knowledge of our body could be perfect we would know the universe. But even the very best of doctors and *hakims* and *vaids* have not been able to acquire it. It will not presumptuous for a layman to aspire to it. No one has yet discovered an instrument which can give us any information about the human mind. Scientists have given attractive description of the activities going on within and without the body, but no one can say what sets the wheel going. Who can explain the why and wherefore of death or foretell its time? In short, after infinite reading and writing, after infinite experience, man has come to know how little he knows.

> The universe within reflects the universe without

A happy working of the human machine depends upon the harmonious activity of the various component parts. If all these work in an orderly manner, the machine runs smoothly. If even one of the essential parts is out of order, it comes to a stop. For instance, if the digestion is out of order, the whole body becomes slack. Therefore, he who takes indigestion and constipation lightly does not know the a-b-c of the rules of health. These two are the root cause of the innumerable ailments.

The question that demands our attention next is : what is the use of human body? Everything in the world can be used and abused. This applies to the body also. We abuse it when we use it for selfish purposes, for self-indulgence or in order to harm another. It is put to its right use if we exercise self-restraint and dedicate ourselves to the service of the whole world. The human soul is the part of the universal spirit of God. When all our activities are directed towards the realization of this link, the body becomes a temple worthy for the spirit to live in.

The body has been described as a mine of dirt. Looked at in its proper perspective, there is no exaggeration in this statement. If the body was nothing else but this, there could be no point in taking such pains to look after it. But if this so-called mine of dirt can be put to its proper use, it becomes our first duty to cleanse it and keep it in a fit condition. The mines of precious stones and gold also have the look of ordinary earth on the surface. The knowledge that there are gold and precious stones underneath, induces men to spend millions and engage scientific brains in order to get at what lies in those mines. Similarly, we cannot take too much pains over keeping in a fit condition the temple of the spirit—the human body.

Man came into the world in order to pay off the debt owed by him to it, that is to say, in order to serve God and His creation. Keeping this point of view in front of him, man acts as a guardian of his body. It becomes his duty to take such care of his body as to enable it to practise the idea of serving to the best of its ability.

2

AIR

No one can live without air as one can without water for a few days and without food much longer. Therefore, nature has surrounded us with air on all sides so that we can get it without any effort.

We take in air through our nose into our lungs. The lungs act as a sort of bellows. The atmospheric air which we breathe in has a life-giving substance—a gas known as oxygen. The air that we breathe out contains poisonous gases. These can kill us if they are not immediately allowed to spread out and get diluted by the atmospheric air. Hence the necessity of proper ventilation.

The air comes into close contact with blood in the lungs and purifies it. Many people do not know the act of breathing. This defect prevents an adequate purification of their blood. Some people breathe through their mouth instead of their nose. This is a bad habit. Nature has so designed the nose that it acts as a sort of filter for the ingoing air and also warms it. In mouth breathers the atmospheric air reaches the lungs without the preliminary filtration or warming. It follows therefore that those who do not know how to breathe should take breathing exercises. They are as easy to learn as are useful. I do not wish to go into a discussion of the various asanas or postures. I do not mean to say that these are not important or useful. But I do wish to emphasize that a well-regulated life outweighs the advantage of studying elaborate postures that ensure breathing through the nose and free chest expansion is enough for our purposes.

If we keep the mouth tightly closed, the breathing would have to be carried out by the nose. Just as we wash our mouth every morning, the nose should be also be cleaned. Clean water, cold or lukewarm water is the best agent for this purpose. It should be taken in a cup in the palm of the hand and draw up through the nostrils. It is possible to draw the water up through one nostril, the other remains closed, and expel in through the other by opening it and closing the former. The process should be carried out gently so as to avoid discomfort. In order to cleanse the back portion of the nose known as nasopharynx, water should be brought out by the mouth or even swallowed.

We must see that the air that we breathe in is fresh. It is good to cultivate a habit of sleeping in the open under the stars. The fear of catching a chill could be dismissed from the mind. Cold can be kept out by plenty of covering. This covering should not extend beyond the neck. If cold is felt on the head, it can be covered with separate piece of cloth. The opening of the respiratory passage—the nose—should never be covered up.

The day clothes should be changed for loose night clothes before retiring. As a matter of fact no clothes are necessary at night when one sleeps covered with a sheet. Tight-fitting clothes should be avoided even during day.

The atmospheric air around us is not always pure, neither it is the same in every country. The choice of the country does not always lie in our hands but the choice of a suitable house in a suitable locality does rest with us till some extent. The general rule should be to live in a locality which is not too congested and insist upon the house being well lighted and well-ventilated.

3

WATER

Next to air, water is the necessity of life. We cannot live without it for more than a few days, just as without air we cannot live for more than a few minutes. Therefore, as in the case of the air, nature has provided us with ample amount of water. Man cannot live on barren land where vast tracts of desert land lie utterly uninhabited.

In order to keep healthy, everyone should take 5lbs. of water or other liquid food in 24 hours. Drinking water must be pure. In many places it is difficult to get pure water. There is always risk in drinking well water. The water of shallow wells, and even deep wells with staircase leading down to the water level, should be considered absolutely unfit for drinking purposes. The difficulty is that the appearance and even the taste of water are no guide to its purity. Water which appears perfectly harmless to look at and to taste, can act as poison. The old custom of not drinking from an unknown well or from a stranger's house is worth copying.

In Bengal almost every house has a *kachcha* tank attached to it. As a rule the water of these is unfit for drinking purpose.

> The appearance and even the taste of water are no guide to its purity

River water is also frequently not fit for drinking, particularly where the river is used for navigation or where it passes by a big city and receives its drainage and sewage water.

In spite of what I have said, I know there are millions of people who have to drink what I have described as impure water. But that does not mean that their example is worth copying. Nature has provided us with sufficient reserves of vitality. But for that, man would have long ago disappeared from the face of the earth because of his own mistakes and transgressions of the rules of health.

> Nature has provided us with sufficient reserves of vitality

Here we are concerned merely with the role of water with regards to health. Whenever we are doubtful about the purity of water, it should be boiled before drinking. In practice it amounts to this that everyone should carry his drinking water with him. Many orthodox Hindus in India do not drink water whilst travelling on account of religious prejudices. Surely, the enlightened can do for the sake of health what the unenlightened do in the name of religion!

4

FOOD

Whilst it is true that man cannot live without air and water, the thing that nourishes the body is food. Hence the saying, food is life.

Food can be divided into three categories : vegetarian, flesh and mixed. Flesh food includes fowl and fish. Milk is an animal product and cannot by any means be included in a strictly vegetarian diet. It serves the purpose of meat to a very large extent. In medical language it is classified as animal food. A layman does not consider milk to be an animal food. On the other hand eggs are regarded by the layman as a flesh food. In reality, they are not. Nowadays sterile eggs are also produced. The hen is not allowed to see the cock and yet it lays eggs. A sterile egg never evolves into a chick. Therefore, he who can take milk should have no objection to take sterile eggs.

Medical opinion is mostly in favour of a mixed diet, although there is a growing school, which is strongly of the opinion that anatomical and physiological evidence is in favour of man being a vegetarian. His teeth, his stomach, intestines etc., seem to prove that nature has meant man to be a vegetarian.

Vegetarian diet besides grains, pulses, edible roots, tubers and leaves, includes fruits, both fresh and dry. Dry fruits include nuts like almonds, pistachio, walnut etc.

I have always been in favour of pure vegetarian diet. But experience has taught me that in order to be perfectly fit, vegetarian diet must include milk and milk-products such as curd, butter, ghee, etc. This is a significant departure from my original idea.

> To be perfectly fit, vegetarian diet must include milk and milk-products

I excluded milk from my diet for six years. At that time, I felt none the worse for the denial. But in year 1917, as a result of my ignorance, I was laid down with severe dysentery. I was reduced to a skeleton, but I stubbornly refused to take any medicine and with equal stubbornness refused to take milk or buttermilk. But I could not build up my body and pick up sufficient strength to leave the bed. I had taken a vow of not taking milk. A medical friend suggested that at the time of taking a vow, I could have in my mind only the milk of cow and buffalo; why would the vow prevent me from taking goat's milk? My wife supported him and I yielded. Really speaking, for one who has given up milk, though at the time of taking the vow only the cow and the buffalo were in mind, milk should be taboo. All animal milks have practically the same composition, though the proportion of the components varies in each case. So I may be said to have kept merely the letter, not the spirit, of the vow. Be that as it may, goat's milk was produced immediately and I drank it. It seemed to bring me new life. I picked up rapidly and was soon able to leave the bed. On account of this and several similar experiences, I have been forced to admit the necessity of adding milk to the strict vegetarian diet. But I am convinced that in the vast vegetable kingdom there must be some kind, which, while supplying those necessary substances which we derive from milk and meat, is free from their drawbacks, ethical and other.

In my opinion there are definite drawbacks in taking milk or meat. In order to get meat we have to kill. And we are certainly not entitled to any other milk except the mother's milk in our infancy. Over and above the moral drawback, there are others, purely from the point of view of health. Both milk and meat bring with them the defects of the animal from which they are derived. Domesticated cattle are hardly ever perfectly healthy. Just like man, cattle suffer from innumerable diseases. Several of these are over-looked even when the cattle are subjected to periodical medical examinations. Besides, medical examination of all the cattle in India seems to be an impossible feat, at any rate for the present. I am conducting a dairy at the Sevagram Ashram. I can easily get help from medical friends. Yet I cannot say with certainty that all the cattle in the Sevagram Dairy are healthy. On the contrary, a cow that had been considered to be healthy by everybody was found to be suffering from tuberculosis. Before this diagnosis was made, the milk of that cow had been used regularly in the Ashram. The Ashram also takes milk from the farmers in the neighbourhood. Their cattle had not been medically examined. It is difficult to determine whether a particular specimen of milk is safe for consumption or not. We have to rest content with as much safety as boiling of the milk can assure us of. If the Ashram cannot boast of fool-proof medical examination of its cattle, and be certain of the safety of its dairy products, the situation elsewhere is not likely to be much better. What applies to the milch cattle applies to a much greater extent to the animals slaughtered for meat. As a general rule, man just depends upon luck to escape from such risks. He does not seem to worry much about his health. He considers himself to be quite safe in his medical fortress in the shape of doctors, *vaids* and *hakims*. His main worry and concern is how to get wealth and position in society. This worry overshadows all the rest. Therefore, so long as some selfless scientist does not, as a result of patient research work, discover a vegetable substitute for milk and meat, man will go on taking meat and milk.

Now let us consider mixed diet. Man requires food which supplies tissue building substances to provide for the growth and daily wear and tear of the body. It should also contain something which can supply energy, fat, certain salts and roughage to help the excretion of waste matter. Tissue building substances are known as proteins. They are obtained from milk, meat, eggs, pulses and nuts. The proteins contained in milk and meat, in other words, the animal proteins being more digestible and assimilable, are much valuable than vegetable proteins. Milk is superior to meat. The medicos tell us that in cases when meat cannot be digested, milk is digested quite easily. For vegetarians milk being the only source of animal proteins, is a very important article of diet. The proteins in raw eggs are considered to be the most easily digestible of all proteins.

But everybody cannot afford to drink milk. And milk is not available in all places. I would like to mention here a very important fact with regards to milk. Contrary to the popular belief, skimmed milk is a very valuable article of diet. There are times when it proves even more useful than whole milk. The chief function of milk is to supply animal proteins for tissue building and tissue repair. Skimming while it partially removes the fats, does not affect the proteins at all. Moreover, the available skimming instrument cannot remove all the fats from milk. Neither there is any likelihood of such an instrument being constructed.

> The chief function of milk is to supply animal proteins for tissue building and tissue repair

The body requires other things besides milk, whole or skimmed. I give the second place to cereals—wheat, rice, jowar, bajra etc. These are used as the staple diet. Different cereals are used as staples in different provinces in India. In many places, more than one kind of cereals are eaten at the same time, for instance, small quantities of wheat, bajra and rice are often served together. This mixture is not necessary for the nourishment of the body. It makes it difficult to regulate the quantity of food intake, and puts an extra strain upon digestion. As all these varieties supply starch mainly, it is better to take one only, at a time. Wheat may well be described as the king among the cereals. If we glance at the world map, we find that wheat occupies the first place. From the point

> Wheat may well be described as the king among the cereals

of view of health, if we can get wheat, rice and other cereals become unnecessary. If wheat is not available and jowar, etc. cannot be taken on account of dislike or difficulty in digesting them, rice has to be resorted to.

The cereals should be properly cleansed, ground on a grinding stone, and the resulting flour used as it is. Sieving of the flour should be avoided. It is likely to remove the *bhusi* or the pericarp which is a rich source of salt and vitamins, both of which are most valuable from the point of view of nutrition. The pericarp also supplies roughage, which helps the action of the bowels. Rice grain being very delicate, nature has provided it with an outer covering or epicure. This is not edible. In order to remove this inedible portion, rice has to be pounded. Pounding should be just sufficient to remove the epicarp or the outer skin of the rice grain. But machine pounding not only removes the outer skin, but also polishes the rice by removing its pericarp. The explanation of the popularity of polished rice lies in the fact that polishing helps preservation. The pericarp is very sweet and unless it is removed, rice is easily attracted by certain organisms. Polished rice and wheat without its pericarp, supply us with almost pure starch. Important constituents of the cereals are lost with the removal of their pericarp. The pericarp of the rice is sold as rice polishings. This and the pericarp of wheat can be cooked and eaten by themselves. They can also be made into *chapatis* or cakes. It is possible that rice *chapatis* may be more easily digestible than whole rice and in this form a lesser quantity may result in full satisfaction.

We are in the habit of dipping each morsel of *chapati* in vegetable or *daal* gravy before eating. The result is that most people swallow their food without proper mastication. Mastication is an important step in the process of digestion, especially that of starch. Digestion of starch begins on its coming into contact with saliva in the mouth. Mastication ensures a thorough mixing of food with saliva. Therefore, starchy food should be eaten in a relatively dry form, which results in a greater flow of saliva and also necessitates their thorough mastication.

After the starch supplying cereals come the protein-supplying pulses-beans, lentils etc. Almost everybody seems to think that pulses are essential constituent of diet. Even meat eaters should have pulses. It is easy to understand that those who have to do hard manual work and who cannot afford to drink milk, cannot do without pulses. But I can say without any hesitation whatsoever that those who follow sedentary occupations as for instance, clerks, business men, doctors and those who are not too poor to buy milk, do not require pulses. Pulses are generally considered to be difficult to digest and are eaten in a much smaller quantity than cereals.

> Those who have to do hard manual work and who cannot afford to drink milk, cannot do without pulses

Out of variety of pulses, peas, gram and haricot beans are considered to be the most and *moong* (green grams) and *masoor* (lentils) the least difficult to digest.

Vegetables and fruits should come third on our list. One would expect them to be cheap and easily available in India. But it is not so. They are generally considered to be delicacies meant for the city people. In the villages fresh vegetable are a rarity, and in most places fruits are also not available. This shortage of greens and fruits is a slur on the administration of India. The villagers can grow plenty of green vegetables if they wish to. The question of fruits cannot be solved so easily. The land legislation is bad from the villager's standpoint. But I am transgressing.

Among fresh vegetables, a fare amount of leafy vegetables must be taken everyday. I do not include potatoes, sweet potatoes, saran etc, which supply starch mainly, among vegetables. They should be put down in same category as starch supplying cereals. A fair helping of ordinary fresh vegetables is advisable. Certain varieties such as cucumber, tomatoes, mustard and cress and other tender leaves need not be cooked. They should be washed properly and eaten raw in small quantities.

As for fruits, our daily diet should include available fruits of the season, e.g. mangoes, grapes etc. should all be used in their season. The best time for taking fruits is in early morning. A breakfast of fruits and milk should give full satisfaction. Those who take an early lunch may have a breakfast of fruits only. Banana is a good fruit. But as it is very rich in starch, it takes the place of bread. Milk and banana make a perfect meal.

A certain amount of fat is also necessary. This can be had in the form of *ghee* or oil. If *ghee* can be had, oil becomes unnecessary. It is difficult to digest and is not as nourishing as pure *ghee*. An ounce and half of ghee per head per day, should be considered ample to supply the needs of the body. Whole milk is also a source of *ghee*. Those who cannot afford it should take enough oil to supply the need for fat. Among oils, sweet oil, coconut oil, and ground nut oil should be given preference. Oil must be fresh. If available, it is better to use hand-pressed oil. Oil and *ghee* sold in the bazaar are generally quiet useless. It is a matter of great sorrow and shame. But so long as honesty has not become an integral part of business morals, whether through legislation or through education, the individual will have to procure the pure article with patience and diligence. One should never be satisfied to take what one can get, irrespective of its quality. It is far better to do with *ghee* oil altogether than to eat rancid oil and adulterated *ghee*. As in the case of fats, a certain amount of sugar is also necessary. Although sweet fruits supply plenty of sugar, there is no harm in taking one to one and half ounces of sugar, brown or white in a day. If one cannot get sweet fruits sugar may become a necessity. But the undue prominence given to sweet things nowadays is wrong. City folk eat too much of sweet things. Milk puddings, milk sweets and sweets of other kinds are consumed in large quantities. They are all unnecessary and are harmful except when taken in very small quantity. It may be said without any fear of exaggeration that the partake of sweet meals and other delicacies, in a country where the millions do not get an ordinary full meal, is equivalent to robbery.

What applies to sweets, applies with equal force to *ghee* and oil. There is no need to eat food fried in *ghee* or oil. To use *ghee* in making *puris* and *laddus* is thoughtless extravagancy.

Those who are not used to such food cannot eat these things at all. Those who do eat them I have often seen fall ill. Taste is acquired, not born with us. All the delicacies of the world cannot equal the relish, that hunger gives to food. A hungry man will eat a dry piece of bread with the greatest relish, whereas one who is not hungry will refuse the best of sweetmeats.

> All the delicacies of the world cannot equal the relish, that hunger gives to food

Now let us consider how often and how much should one eat. Food should be taken as a matter of duty—even as a medicine—to sustain the body, never for the satisfaction of the palate. Thus, pleasurable feeling comes from satisfaction of real hunger. Therefore, we can say that relish is dependent upon hunger and not outside it. Because of our wrong habits and artificial way of living, very few people know what their system requires. Our parents who bring us into this world do not, as a rule, cultivate self-control. Their habits and their way of living influence the children to a certain extent. The mother's food during pregnancy is bound to affect the child. After that during childhood, the mother pampers the child with all sorts of tasty foods. She gives the child a little bit out of whatever she herself may be eating and the child's digestive system gets a wrong training from its infancy. Habits once formed are difficult to shed. There are very few who succeed in getting rid of them. But when the realization comes to man that he is his own bodyguard, and his body has been dedicated to service, he desires to learn law of keeping his body in a fit condition and tries hard to follow them.

We have now reached a point when we can lay down the amount of various foods required by a man of sedentary habits, which most men and women who read this pages, are.

Cow's milk	2 lbs.
Cereals (wheat, rice, bajra in all)	6 oz.
Vegetable leafy	3 oz.
Vegetable others	5 oz.
Vegetables raw	1 oz.
Ghee	1-1/2 oz.

Butter	2 oz.
White Sugar	1 1/2 oz.

Fresh fruits according to one's taste and purse. In any case it is good to take two sour limes a day. The juice should be squeezed and taken with vegetables or in water, cold or hot. All these weights are of raw stuff. I have not put down the amount of salt. It should be added afterwards according to taste.

Now, how often should one eat? Many people take two meals a day. The general rule is to take three meals: breakfast early in the morning and before going out to work, dinner at midday and supper in the evening or late. There is no necessity to have more than three meals. In cities some people keep on nibbling from time to time. This habit is harmful. The digestive apparatus requires rest.

5

CONDIMENTS

I have not said anything about condiments in the last chapter. Common salt may be rightly counted as the king among condiments. Many people cannot eat their food without it. The body requires certain salts and common salt is one

> Common salt may be rightly counted as the king among condiments

of them. These salts occur naturally in the various foodstuffs but when food is cooked in an unscientific way, e.g., throwing away water in which rice, potatoes, other vegetables have been boiled, the supply becomes inadequate. The deficiency then has to be made up by a separate addition of salt. As common salt is one of the most essential salts for the body, I have said in the last chapter that it might be supplemented in small quantities.

But several condiments are not required by the body as a general rule, e.g., chillies fresh or dry, pepper, turmeric, coriander, caraway, mustard, methi, asafoetida, etc. These are taken just for the satisfaction of the palate. My opinion, based on my personal experience of fifty years, is that not one of them is needed to keep perfectly healthy. Those whose digestion has become very feeble might take these things as medicine for a certain length of time, if considered necessary. But one should make it a point to avoid their use for the satisfaction of the palate. All condiments, even salt, destroy the natural flavour of the foodstuff much more than after the addition of salt or other condiments. That is why I have said that salt should be taken when necessary as an adjunct. As for chillies, they burn the mouth and irritate the stomach. Those who are not in a habit of taking chillies cannot bear them in the beginning. I have seen several cases of sore mouth caused by the taking of chillies. I know of one case who was very fond of chillies, and an excessive use resulted in his premature death. The Negro in South Africa will not touch condiments. He cannot bear the colour of turmeric in his food. In the same way, Englishmen also do not readily take to our condiments.

6

TEA, COFFEE AND COCOA

None of these is required by the body. The use of tea is said to have originated in China. It has a special use in that country. As a rule one cannot rely on the purity of drinking water in China and therefore it must be boiled before use to ensure safety. Some clever Chinaman discovered a grass called tea which when added to boiled water in a very small quantity gave it a golden colour. The colour did not appear unless the water was really boiled. Thus the grass became an infallible test for seeing when a given quantity of water was boiled. The way, the test is used, is to put the tea leaves in a strainer. If the water is boiled it will assume a golden colour. Another quality of tea leaves is said to be that they impart a delicate flavour to the water.

Tea prepared as above is harmless. But the tea that is generally prepared and taken has not only nothing to recommend it, it is actually harmful. The leaves contain tannin which is harmful to the body. Tannin is generally used in the tanneries to harden leather. When taken internally it produces a similar effect upon the mucous lining of the stomach and intestine. This impairs digestion and cause dyspepsia. It is said that in England innumerable women suffer from various ailments on account of their habit of drinking tea which contains tannin. Habitual tea drinkers begin to feel restless if they do not get their cup at the usual time. In my opinion, the usefulness of tea, if any, consists in the fact that it supplies a warm sweet drink which contains some milk. The same purpose may well be served by taking boiled hot water mixed with a little milk and sugar.

What I have said about tea applies more or less to coffee also. There is a popular saying about coffee in Hindustani which say, "Coffee allays cough and relieves flatulence, but it impairs physical and sexual vigour and makes blood watery, so that there are three disadvantages against its two advantages." I do not know how far the saying is justified.

I hold similar opinion with regard to cocoa. Those whose digestion works normally, do not require the help of tea, coffee or cocoa. A healthy man can get all the satisfaction that he needs out of ordinary food. I have freely partaken of all the three. I used to suffer from one ailment or another while I was using them. By giving them up I have lost nothing, and have benefited a good deal. I can get the same satisfaction from a clear vegetable soup that I used to derive from tea etc. Hot water, honey and lemon make a healthy nourishing drink, which can well substitute tea or coffee.

> *Hot water, honey and lemon make a healthy nourishing drink, which can well substitute tea or coffee*

7

INTOXICANTS

The intoxicants used in India might be taken as the following: alcohol, *bhang*, *ganja*, tobacco and opium. Alcohol or liquor include the country-made liquor and arak, besides the large quantity of liquor imported from foreign countries. All these should be strictly prohibited. Alcohol makes a man forget himself and while its effects last, he becomes utterly incapable of doing anything useful. Those who take to drinking, ruin themselves and ruin their people. They lose all sense of decency and propriety.

There is a school who favours limited and regulated consumption of alcohol and believe it to be useful. I have not found any weight in their argument. Even if we accept their view for a moment, we have still to face the fact that innumerable human beings cannot be kept under discipline. Therefore it becomes our duty to prohibit alcoholic drinks even if it were only for the sake of this vast majority.

Parsis have strongly supported the use of *tadi*. They say that although *tadi* is an intoxicant it is also a food and even helps to digest other foodstuffs. I have carefully examined this argument and have read a fair amount of literature pertaining to this subject. But I have been a witness of the terrible straits to which *tadi* reduces the poor and therefore I have come to the conclusion that it can have no place in man's food.

The advantages, attributed to *tadi*, are all available from other foodstuffs. Tadi is made out of *khanjur* juice. Fresh *khanjur* juice is not an intoxicant. It is known as *nira* in Hindustani and many people have been cured of their constipation as a result of drinking *nira*. I have taken it myself though it did not act as a laxative with me. I found that it had the same food value as sugarcane juice. If one drinks a glass of *nira* in the morning instead of drinking tea, etc., he should not need any thing for breakfast. As in the case of sugarcane juice, palm juice can be boiled to make jaggery. *Khanjuri* is a variety of palm tree. Several varieties of palm grow spontaneously in our country. All of them yield drinkable juice. As *nira* gets fermented very quickly, it has to be used up immediately and therefore on the spot. Since this condition is difficult to fulfill except to a limited extent, in practice, the best use of *nira* is to convert it into palm jaggery. Palm jaggery can well replace sugarcane jaggery. In fact some people prefer it to the latter. One advantage of palm jaggery over sugarcane jaggery is that it is less sweet and therefore one can eat more of it. The All Indian Village Association has done a great deal to popularize palm jaggery, but much remains to be done. If the palms that are used for making *tadi* are used for making jaggery, India will never lack sugar and the poor will be able to get good jaggery for very little money. Palm jaggery can be converted into molasses and refined sugar. But the jaggery is much more useful than refined sugar. The salts present in the jaggery are lost in the process of refining. Just as refined wheat flour and polished rice lose some of their nutritive value because of the loss of the pericarp, refined sugar also loses some of the nutritive value of the jaggery. One may generalize that all foodstuffs are richer if taken in their natural state as far as possible.

> All foodstuffs are richer if taken in their natural state as far as possible

None of the public workers perhaps has the same bitter experience of the evils of the drinking as I have had. In South Africa, most of the Indians going there as indentured labourers

32 *Key to Health*

were addicted to drinking. The law there did not in my time permit Indians to take liquor to their houses except under a medical certificate. They could go to the drinking booths and drink as much as they liked. Even the women had fallen victims to this evil habit. I have seen them in the most pathetic condition. One who has seen those scenes near the public bars will never support drinking.

African Negroes were not given to drinking originally. Liquor may be said to have simply ruined them. Large numbers of Negro labourers are seen to waste all their earnings in drinking so that their lives become devoid of any grace.

And what about Englishmen? I have seen respectable Englishmen falling in the gutter under the effect of alcohol. There is no exaggeration in this statement. During the war many Englishmen had to leave the Transvaal. Some of them were taken in my home. One of them was an engineer and a good man in every way, when not under the effects of alcohol. He was a theosophist. Unfortunately, he was addicted to drink and lost all control over himself when he was drunk. He tried hard to give up the habit, but as far as I know he never succeeded.

On my return from South Africa to India I had a similar painful experience of the evils of drink. Several princes have been and are being ruined by liquor. What applies to them applies more or less to many a rich youth. The condition of labour as a result of taking alcohol is also pitiable. That, as a result of such bitter experience, I have become a staunch opponent of alcohol, will not surprise the readers.

In a nut shell, alcohol ruins one physically, morally, intellectually and economically.

8

OPIUM

The criticism levelled against alcohol applies equally to opium, although the two are very different in their action. Under the effect of alcohol a person becomes rowdy, whereas opium makes the addict dull and lazy. He becomes even drowsy and incapable of doing anything useful. The evil effect of alcohol strikes the eyes everyday, but those of opium are not so glaring. Anyone wishing to see its devastating effect should go to Assam or Orissa. Thousands have fallen victim to this intoxicant, in those provinces. They give one the impression of living on the verge of death.

But China is said to have suffered the most from the evils of opium. The Chinese possess a better physique than the Indians. But Chinese addicted to opium look miserable and more dead than alive. An opium addict will stoop to anything in order to procure his dose of opium.

Several years ago, what is known as Opium War took place between China and Great Britain. China did not wish to buy opium from India. But the English wanted to impose it on China. India was also to blame in that several Indians had taken opium contracts in India. The trade paid well and the treasury received crores of rupees as opium revenue. This was obviously an immoral trade and yet it went on flourishing. Finally, as a result of a mighty agitation in England, it was stopped. A thing of this type, which simply ruins people, should not be tolerated for a single minute.

After having had my say on opium as an intoxicant, I must admit that its place in Material Medic is incontestable. It is impossible to do without this drug as medical agent. But that can be no reason for using it as an intoxicant. Opium is a well-known poison and its use as an intoxicant should be strictly prohibited.

9

TOBACCO

Tobacco has simply worked havoc among mankind. Once caught in its tangle, it is rare to find anyone get out again. The use of tobacco is prevalent all over the world in one form or another. Tolstoy has called it the worst of all intoxicants. This verdict of that great man should command our attention and respect. He had freely indulged in the use of tobacco and alcohol in his early days and was familiar with the harmful effects of both. I must admit, however, that in spite of this, I cannot talk about the evils of tobacco with the same authority and knowledge as in the case of opium and alcohol. But I can certainly say that I am not aware of a single advantage occurring from the use of tobacco. Smoking is an expensive habit. I know of an Englishman who used to spend five pounds, i.e., seventy-five rupees on tobacco every month. His monthly earning was twenty-five pounds, so that he smoked away one fifth of his monthly income.

Tobacco smokers become callous and careless of others' feeling. Non-smokers generally cannot bear the smell of tobacco smoke, but one often comes across people in railway trains and tramways who just go on smoking, heedless of the

> *Tobacco smokers become callous and careless of others' feelings*

feelings of their neighbours. Smoking causes salivation and most smokers have no hesitation in spitting anywhere.

Tobacco smokers' mouths emit a foul smell. Probably tobacco kills the finer feelings and perhaps it is to this end that men take to smoking. There is no doubt that tobacco is an intoxicant and while under its effects one forgets one's worries and misfortunes. One of Tolstoy's characters had to do a ghastly deed. Tolstoy makes him drink liquor at first. The man was to murder someone. In spite of the effects of liquor, he hesitated to do so. Lost in thought he lights a cigar and begins to smoke. As he watches the smoke curling up he exclaims, "What a coward I am! When it is my duty to commit this murder, why should I hesitate to do so ? Get up, go ahead, and do your job." Thus his wavering mind finally decides to commit it. I know, this argument is not very convincing. All smokers are not bad men. I know that millions of smokers seem to live ordinary straightforward lives. All the same the thoughtful should ponder above quotation. What Tolstoy perhaps means is that smoker keeps on committing minor crimes which generally pass unnoticed.

In India people use tobacco for smoking, snuffing and also for chewing. Some believe that snuff produces a beneficial effect, and they use it under the advise of *vaids* and *hakims*. I think that it is not necessary. A healthy man should never have such requirements.

As for chewing tobacco, it is the dirtiest of all the three ways in which tobacco is used. I have always maintained that its usefulness is a mere figment of the imagination. I have found no reasons to change my opinion. There is a popular saying in Gujrati which says, all the three are equally guilty: the smoker fills his house with smoke, the chewer dirties every corner and the snuffer his clothes.

Tobacco chewers, if they are sensible, keep a spittoon at hand. But the vast majority spit on the floor, in the corners and on the wall unabashed. The smoker fills his house with smoke and runs the risk of it catching fire, and he who takes snuff soils his clothes. If there are any who keep handkerchief and thus save their clothes from soiling, they are exception that prove the general rule. Lovers of health, if they are slaves to any of these evil habits, will resolutely get out of the slavery. Several people are addicted to one, two or all the three of these habits.

They do not appear loathsome to them. But if we think over it calmly, there is nothing becoming about blowing of smoke or keeping the mouth stuffed with tobacco and chew practically the whole day long or opening a snuffbox and taking snuff every now and then. All the three are most dirty habits.

10

BRAHMACHARYA

Brahmacharya literally means that mode of life which leads to the realization of God. That realization is impossible without practising self-restraint. Self-restraint means restraint of all the senses. But ordinarily brahmacharya is understood to mean control of sexual organs and prevention of seminal discharge through complete control over the sexual instinct and the sexual organs. This becomes natural for the man who exercises self-restraint all round. It is only when observance of brahmacharya becomes natural to one that he or she derives the greatest benefit from it. Such a person should be free from anger and kindhearted passion. The so-called brahmacharis, that one generally comes across, behave as if their one occupation in life was the display of bad temper.

One notices that these people disregard the ordinary rules of brahmacharya and merely aim at and expect to prevent seminal discharges. They fail to achieve their object. Some of them become almost insane while others betray a sickly appearance. They are unable to prevent the discharge and if they succeed in restraining themselves from sexual intercourse, they think that they have attained all that was needed. Now mere abstention from sexual intercourse cannot be termed brahmacharya. So long as the desire for intercourse is there, one cannot be said to have attained brahmacharya. Only he who has burnt away sexual desire in its entirely may be said to have attained control over his sexual organs. The absence of seminal discharges is a straightforward result of brahmacharya, but is not all. There is something very striking about a full-fledged brahmachari. His speech, his thought, and his action, all bespeak possession of vital force.

Such a brahmachari do not flee from the company of women. He may not hanker after it nor may he avoid it even when it means rendering of necessary survive. For him the distinction between men and women almost disappears. No one should distort my words and use them as an argument in favour of licentiousness. What I mean to say is that, a man whose sexual desire has been burnt up ceases to make a distinction between men and women. It must be so. His conception of beauty alters. He will not look at the external form. He or she whose character is beautiful will be beautiful in his eyes. Therefore, the sight of women called beautiful will not ruffle or excite him. Even his sexual organs will begin to look different. In other words, such a man has so controlled his sexual instinct that he never gets erections. He does not become impotent for lack of the necessary secretions of sexual glands. But these secretions in his case are sublimated into a vital force pervading his whole being. It is said that an important man is not free form sexual desire. Some of my correspondents belonging to this group tell me that they desire erection but they fail to get it and yet have seminal discharges. Such men have either become impotent or are on the way to become so for loss of the necessary secretions. This is a pitiable state. But the cultivated impotency of the man, whose sexual desire has been burnt up and whose sexual secretion are being converted into vital force, is wholly different. It is to be desired by everybody. It is true that such a brahmachari is rare to find.

I took the vow of brahmacharya in 1906. In other words, my efforts to become a perfect brahmachari started 36 years ago. I cannot say I have attained the full brahmacharya of my definition, but in my opinion I have made substantial progress towards it. If God wills it, I might attain even perfection in this life. Anyway, there is no relaxation of efforts nor is there any despondence in me. I do not consider 36 years too long a period for effort. The richer the prize, the richer the effort must be. Meanwhile, my ideas regarding the necessity for brahmacharya have become stronger. Some of my experiments have not reached a stage when they might be placed before the public with advantage. I hope to do so some day if they succeed to my satisfaction. Success might make the attainment of brahmacharya comparatively easier.

> The richer the prize, the richer the effort must be

But the brahmacharya on which I wish to lay emphasis in this chapter is limited to the conservation of sexual secretions. The glorious fruit of perfect brahmacharya is not to be had from the observance of this limited brahmacharya. But no one can reach perfect brahmacharya without reaching the limited variety.

And maintenance of perfect health should be considered almost an utter impossibility without the brahmacharya leading to the conservation of the sexual secretions. To countenance wastage of a secretion which has the power of creating another human being is, to say the least, an indication of gross ignorance. A firm grasp of the fact that semen is meant to be used only for procreation and not for self-indulgence, leaves no room whatsoever for indulging in animal passion. Assimilation of the knowledge that the vital fluid is never meant for waste should restrain men and women from becoming crazy over sexual intercourse.

> Marriage ought to signify a union of heart between two partners

Marriage will then come to have a different significance and the way it is treated at present will appear disgusting. Marriage ought to signify a union of heart between two partners. A married couple is worthy of being considered dared brahmacharis if they never think of sexual intercourse except for the purposes of procreation. Such an intercourse is not possible unless both parties desire it. It will never be

Brahmacharya 41

restored to in order to satisfy passion without the desire for a child. after intercourse which has been performed as a matter of duty, the desire to repeat the process should never arise.

What I am saying may not be taken as copy book wisdom. The reader should know that I am writing this after a long personal experience. I know that what I am writing is contrary to the common practice. But in order to make progress we have often to go beyond the limits of common experience. Great discoveries have been possible only as a result of challenging the common experience or commonly held beliefs. The invention of the simple match stick was challenged to the common experience and the discovery of electricity confounded all preconceived notions.

What is true of physical thing is equally true of things spiritual. In the early days there was no such thing as marriage. Men and women, as in the case of animals, mated promiscuously. Self-restraint was unknown. Some advanced men went beyond the rut of common practice and discover the law of self-restraint. It is our duty to investigate the hidden possibilities of the law of self-restraint. Therefore, when I say it is the duty of every man and woman to take the marital relations to the state indicated by me it is not to be dismissed as utterly impracticable. If human life is moulded as it ought to be, conservation of vital fluid can become a natural thing for everyone.

The sexual glands are all the time secreting the semen. This secretion should be utilized for enhancing one's mental, physical and spiritual energy. He, who would learn to utilize it thus, will find that he requires very little food to keep his body in a fit condition. And yet he will be as capable as any of undertaking physical labour. Mental exertion will not tire him easily nor will he show the ordinary signs of old age. Just as a ripe fruit or an old leaf falls off naturally, so will such a brahmachari when his times comes pass away with all his faculties intact. Although with the passage of time the effects of the natural wear and tear must be manifest in his body, his intellects instead of showing signs of decay should show progressive clarity. If all this is correct, the real key to health lies in the conservancy of vital energy.

I gave here the rules for the conservation of vital force as I know them.

1. Sexual desire has its root in one's thought. Therefore, complete control over thought is necessary. The way to achieve it is this. Never let your mind remain idle. Keep it filled with good and useful ideas. In other words keep thinking of whatever duty you have on hand. There need be no worry about it, but think out how you can become an expert in your department and then put your thoughts into action. There should be no waste of thoughts. *Japa* (repetition of God's name) is a great support when ideal thoughts haunt you. Contemplate God in the form you have pictured Him unless you know Him as formless. While *japa* is going on, no other thoughts should be allowed to enter one's mind. This is the ideal state. But if one cannot reach it and all sorts of uninvited thoughts invade one's mind, one should not become disheartened. *Namajapa* should be continued faithfully and in the confidence that ultimate victory is bound to follow.

2. As with our thoughts, so with our reading and talking. These should be healthy and clean. Erotic literature should be avoided. Idle, indecent talk leads to indecent action. It is obvious that one who does not wish to feed his animal passions will avoid occupations which tend to include them.

3. Like the mind, the body must also be kept well and usefully occupied, so that the fatigue of the day may lead to refreshing dreamless sleep. As far as possible, work should

> **Laziness is the enemy of self-restraint**

be in open. Those who for some reason or the other, cannot undertake physical labour, should make it a point to do regular exercise. In my opinion, a brisk walk in the open is the best form of exercise. During the walk the mouth should be closed and breathing should be done through the nose. Sitting or walking, the body must be held erect. To sit or stand otherwise is a sign of laziness and laziness is the enemy of self-restraint. Yogic exercises—*asanas*—are also useful. This much I can say from my personal experience that one who keeps his hands and feet, eyes and ears, healthily occupied does not have much difficulty in controlling the animal appetite. Everyone can test this for himself.

4. A Sanskrit text say that a man becomes what he eats. A glutton who exercises no restraint in eating is a slave to his animal passions. One who has not been able to control his palate, will never be able to control the other senses. If this is true, it is clear that one should take just enough food for the requirements of the body and no more. The diet should be healthy and well-balanced. The body was never meant to be treated as a refuse bin holding the foods that the palate demands. Food is meant to sustain the body. This body has been given to man as a means of self-realization. Self-realization means realization of God. A person who has made this realization the object of his or her life, will never become a slave to the animal passion.

5. Man should look upon every woman as his mother, sister or daughter. No one ever entertains impure thoughts with regard to his mother, sister or daughter. Similarly, women should look upon every man as her father, brother or son.

I have given more hints than these in my other writing, but they are all contained in the five given above. Anyone who observes them should find it easy to overcome what has been called the greatest of all passions. A person, who has real desire for brahmacharya, will not give up the effort because he or she regards the observance of these rules as impossible or at least within the reach of one in a million. The effort is a joy in itself. To put it in another way, the joy of possessing perfect health is not to be compared with any other, and perfect health is unattainable by slaves. Slavery of one's animality is perhaps the worst of all.

A few words about contraceptives will not be out of place here. The practice of preventing progeny, by means of artificial methods, is not a new thing. In the past such methods were practised secretly and they were crude. Modern society have given them respectable place and made improvements. They have been given a philanthropic garb. The advocates of contraceptives say that sexual desire is a natural instinct—some call it a blessing. They therefore say that it is not right to suppress the desire even if it were possible. Birth control by means of self-restraint is, in their opinion, difficult to practise. If a substitute for self-restraint is not prescribed, the health of innumerable is bound to suffer through frequent pregnancies. They add that if births are not regulated, over-population will ensue; individual families will be pauperized and their children will be ill-fed, ill-clothed and ill educated. Therefore, they argue, it is the duty of scientists to devise harmless and effective methods of birth control. This argument has failed to convince me. The use of contraceptives is likely to produce evils of which we have no conception. But the worse danger is that the use of contraceptives kills the desire for self-restraint. In my opinion it is too heavy a price to pay for any possible immediate gain. But this is not the place to argue my point. Those who would like to pursue this subject further should procure the booklet called Self-Restraint v. Self Indulgence and read what I have said therein and then do as their heads and heart may decide. Those who have not the desire or the leisure to read booklet will, if they follow my advice, avoid contraceptive as poison. They should try their best to exercise self-restraint. They should take up such activities as would keep their bodies and minds fully occupied and give a suitable outlet to their energy. It is necessary to have some healthy recreation when one is tired by physical labour. There should not be a single

> *Man must understand that woman is his companion and helpmate in life and not the means of satisfying his carnal desire*

moment of idleness for the devil to creep in. In this way, true conjugal love will be established and directed into healthy channels. Both the partners will make a progressive rise in their moral height. The joy of true renunciation, once they come to know it, will prevent them from turning to animal enjoyment. Self-deception is the greatest stumbling block. Instead of controlling the mind, the fountain of all animal desires, men and women involve themselves in the vain endeavour to avoid the physical act. If there is a determination to control the thought and the action, victory is sure to follow. Man must understand that woman is his companion and helpmate in life and not the means of satisfying his carnal desire. There must be a clear perception that the purpose of human creation was wholly different from that of the satisfaction of the animal wants.

SECTION II

Natural Therapeutics

❋ ❋ ❋

Disease springs from a wilful or ignorant breach of the laws of nature

11

EARTH

These chapters are written in order to introduce the reader to this most important branch of therapeutics and tell him how I have made use of these methods in my own life. The subject has been touched upon in the foregoing chapters. It will be dealt here. The science of natural therapeutics is based on a use, in the treatment of disease, of the same five elements which constitute the human body. To refresh the reader's memory, these are earth, water, ether, sunlight and air. It is my effort to point out how they can be utilized for health purposes.

Until the year 1901, although I did not rush to doctors whenever I happened to get ill, I did use their remedies to a certain extent. I used to take fruitsalt for constipation. The late Dr. Pranjivan Mehta who had come to Natal introduced me to certain drugs to remove general lassitude. This led me to read literature on the uses of drugs. Add to this a short stay at a cottage hospital in Natal. This enabled me to carry on for some time, but none of the drugs did me any good in the end. Headaches and loss of a sense of general well-being persisted. I was very dissatisfied with this state of things and what little faith I had in medicines began to fade.

All through this interval my experiments in dietetics were

continued. I had great faith in nature cure methods, but there was nobody to help me with practical guidance in their use. With the help of whatever knowledge I could gather by reading little of nature cure literature, I tried to treat myself by diet regulation. My habit of going out for long walks also stood me in good stead, and thanks to that habit I did not have actually to take to bed. While I was thus managing to keep going somehow, Mr. Polak handed me Just's book, called *Return to Nature*. He did not follow Just's instructions himself, except that he tried to regulate his diet more or less according to Just's teaching. But knowing me as he did, he thought I would like the book. Just lays great emphasis on the use of earth. I felt that I ought to give it a try. For constipation, Just advises cold mud poultice on the lower abdomen throughout the night. The result was most satisfactory. I had a natural well-formed motion the next morning and from that day onwards I have hardly ever touched fruitsalt. Occasionally, I feel the need of a purgative and take less than a dessert spoonful of castor oil early in the morning. The mud poultice should be 3 inches broad, 6 inches long and 1 inch thick. Just claims that mud can cure man bitten by a poisonous snake. He would pack wet earth all round the body. I mention this for what it is worth. I would like to put down here what I have tested and proved. Headache may be due to several causes, but whatever the cause, as a general rule, an application of mud poultice relieves it for the time being.

Mud poultices cure ordinary boils. I have applied mud to discharging abscesses as well. For these cases I prepare the poultice by packing the mud in a clean piece of cloth dipped in potassium permanganate lotion. In the majority of cases this treatment results in complete cure. I do not remember a single case in which it has failed me. Mud application immediately relieves the pain of a wasp sting. I have used it in many cases of scorpion bite though with much less success. Scorpions have become a nuisance in Sevagram. We have tried all the known treatments for scorpion bite, but none has proved infallible. I can say this that the results of mud application are not inferior to those of any other form of treatment.

In high fever, an application of mud poultice on the head and abdomen is very useful. Although it does not always bring down the temperature, it does invariably soothe the patient and make him feel better, so that the patients themselves ask for these

> Application of mud poultice on the head and abdomen is very useful

applications. I have used it in several cases of typhoid fever. The fever no doubt runs its own course but mud applications seem to relieve restlessness and abate the suffering. We have had about ten cases of typhoid fever. I have not used any drugs in the treatment of these cases. I have made use of other nature cure methods besides mud poultices, but about those in their own place.

In Sevagram we have made free use of hot mud poultices as substitute for antiphlogistine. A little oil and salt is added to the mud and it is heated sufficiently long to ensure sterilization.

I have not told the reader what kind of earth should be used for mud poultices. In the beginning I used to procure sweet smelling clean red earth. It emits a delicate smell when it is mixed with water. But this kind of earth is not easy to obtain. In a city like Bombay it is a problem to get any kind of earth. It is safe to use soft alluvial clay, which is neither gritty nor sticky. One should never use earth taken from mannured soil. Earth should be dried, pounded, and passed through a fine sieve. If there is any doubt as to its cleanliness, it should be well heated and thus sterilized. Mud used as a poultice on a clean surface need not be thrown away after use. It can be used again and again after drying it in the sun or on fire and pounding and sieving it. I am not aware that mud poultice made out of the same earth again and again as described above, is any the less efficacious. I have myself use it in this way and did not find it any the less efficacious for repeated use. Some friends who regularly used mud poultices tell me that mud from Jumna's banks is particularly good for this purpose.

Eating Earth

Just writes that clean earth may be eaten in order to overcome constipation. Five to ten grams is the maximum dose. The rationale is said to be this. Earth is not disgusted. It acts as roughage and must pass out. The peristalsis thus stimulated pushes out of the fecal matter as well. I have not tried this myself. Therefore those who wish to do so, should try it on their own responsibility. I am inclined to think that a trial or two is not likely to harm anyone.

12

HYDROTHERAPY

Hydrotherapy is a well-known and ancient form of therapy. Many books have been written on the subject, but in my opinion the form of hydrotherapy suggested by Kuhne is simple and effective. Kuhne's book on nature cure is very popular in India. Andhra has the greatest number of Kuhne's followers. He has written a good deal about diet as well, but here I wish to confine myself to his experiments in hydrotherapy.

Hip bath and sitz bath are the most important of Kuhne's contribution to hydrotherapy. He has devised a special tub for use though one can do without it. Any tub thirty to thirty six inches long according to the patient's height generally serves the purpose. Experience will indicate the proper size. The tub should be filled with fresh cold water so that it dose not overflow when the patient sits in it. In summer the water may be iced, if it is not cold enough, to give a gentle shock to the patient. Generally, water kept in earthen jars overnight answers the purpose. Water can also be cooled by putting a piece of cloth on the surface of the water and then fanning it vigorously. The tub should be kept against the bathroom wall and a plank put in the tub to serve as back rest. The patient should sit in the tub keeping his feet outside. Portions of the body outside the water should be kept well covered so that the patient does not feel cold. After the patient is comfortably seated in the tub, gentle friction should be taken for five to thirty minutes. When it is over, the body should be rubbed dry and the patient put to bed.

Hip bath brings down the temperature in high fever and given in the manner described above it never does any harm, and may do much good. It relieves constipation and improves digestion. The patient feels fresh and active after it. In cases of constipation, Kuhne advises a brisk walk for half an hour immediately after the bath. It should never be given on a full stomach.

I have tried hip baths on a fairly large scale. They have proved efficacious in more than 75 cases out of 100. In case of hyperpyrexia, if the patient's condition permits of his being seated in the tub, the temperature immediately invariably falls at least by two to three degrees and, the onset of delirium is averted.

The rationale of the hip bath according to Kuhne is this. Whatever the apparent cause of fever, the real cause in every case is one and the same, i.e. accumulation of waste matter in the intestines. The heat generated by the putrefaction of this waste matter is manifested in the form of fever and several other ailments. Hip bath brings down this internal fever so that fever and other ailments which are the external manifestations thereof subside automatically. How far this reasoning is correct, I cannot say. It is for experts to do so. Although the medical professionals have taken some things from nature cure methods, on the whole they have given cold shoulder to naturopathy. In my opinion both the parties are to be blamed for this state of affairs. The medical professionals have got into the habit of confining themselves to whatever is included in their own curriculum. They present an attitude of indifference, if not that of contempt, for anything that lies

> The medical professionals have got into the habit of confining themselves to whatever is included in their own curriculum

outside their groove. On the other hand, the nature curists nurse a feeling of grievance against the medicos and, in spite of their very limited scientific knowledge they make tall claims. They lack the spirit of organization. Each one is self-satisfied and works by himself instead of all pooling their recourses for the advancement of their system. No one tries to work out in a scientific spirit all the implications and possibilities of the system. No one tries to cultivate humility, (if it is possible to cultivate humility).

I have not said all this in order to belittle the work of the naturopaths. As a lay co-worker I wish them to see things in their true colour so that they may make improvements wherever possible. It is my conviction that so long as some dynamic personality, from among the naturopaths themselves, does not come forward with the zeal of missionary, things will continue as they are. Orthodox medicine has its own science, medical unions and teaching institutions. It has too a certain measure of success. The medical profession should not be expected to put faith, all of a sudden, in things which are yet to be fully tested and scientifically proved.

In the meantime the public should know that the specialty of nature cure methods lies in the fact that being natural, they can be safely practised by laymen. If a man, suffering from headache, wets a piece of cloth in cold water and wraps it round his head, it can do no harm. The addition of earth to cold water enhances the utility of the cold pack.

> **Specialty of nature cure methods lies in the fact that being natural, they can be safely practised by laymen**

Now about the size or friction bath. The organ of reproduction is one of the most sensitive parts of the body. There is something illusive about the sensitiveness of the glans penis and the foreskin. I know not how to describe it. Kuhne has made use of this knowledge for therapeutic purposes. He advises application of gentle friction to the outer end of the external sexual organ by means of a soft wet piece of cloth, while cold water is being poured. In the case of colour. The

Hydrotherapy 55

sheet used for these patients, should afterwards be sterilized by soaking it in boiling water, leaving the sheet in water till it cools down sufficiently and then washed with soap and water.

In cases where circulation has become sluggish, the leg muscles feel sore and there is a peculiar ache and feeling of discomfort in the legs, an ice massage does a lot of good. This treatment is more effective in summer months. Massaging a weak patient with ice in winter might prove a risky affair.

Now a few words about the therapeutics of hot water. An intelligent use of hot water gives relief in many cases. Application of iodine is a very popular remedy for all injuries and the like. Application of hot water will prove equally effective in most of these cases. Tincture of iodine is applied on swollen and bruised areas. Hot water fomentations are likely to give equal relief, if not more. Again, iodine drops are used in cases of earache. Irrigation of the ear with warm water is likely to relieve the pain in most of these cases. The use of iodine is attended with certain risks. The patient may have allergy towards the drug. Iodine mistaken for something else and taken internally might prove disastrous. But there is no risk whatsoever in using hot water. Boiling water is as good a disinfectant as tincture of iodine. I do not mean to belittle the usefulness of iodine. It is one of the few drugs which I regard most useful and necessary, but it is an expensive thing. The poor cannot afford to buy it and moreover its use cannot be safely entrusted to everybody. But water is available everywhere. We may not despise its therapeutic value because it is obtained so easily. Knowledge of common household remedies often proves a godsend in many crises.

In cases of scorpion bite where all remedies have failed, immersion of the part in hot water has been found to relieve the pain to a certain extent.

A shivering fit or a rigour can be made to subside by

putting buckets of hot boiling water all round the patient who is well wrapped up or by saturating the atmosphere of the room with steam by some other device. A rubber hot water bag is a most useful thing, but it is not found in every household. A glass bottle with a well fitting cork, filled with hot water and wrapped in a piece of cloth, serves the same purpose. Care should be taken to choose bottles that will not crack on hot water being poured into them.

> Steam baths are most useful in cases of rheumatism and other joint pains

Steam is a more valuable therapeutic agent. It can be used to make the patient sweat. Steam bath are most useful in cases of rheumatism and other joint pains. The easiest as well as the oldest method of taking steam bath is this. Spread a blanket or two on a sparsely but tightly woven cot and put one or two covered vessels full with boiling water under it. Make the patient lie flat on the cot and cove him up in such a way that ends of the covering blankets touch the ground and thus prevent the steam from escaping and the outside air from getting in. After arranging everything as above, the lid from the vessels containing boiling water is removed and steam soon gets on to the patient lying between the blankets. It may be necessary to change the water once or twice. Usually in India people keep an *angithi* under the pots to keep the water boiling. This ensures continuous discharge of steam, but is attended with risk of accidents. A single spark might set fire to the blankets or to the cot and endanger the patient's life. Therefore, it is advisable to use the method described by me even though it might seem slow and tedious.

Some people add neem leaves or other herbs to the water used for generating steam. I do not know if such an addition increases the efficiency of steam. The object is to induce sweat and that is attained by mere steam.

In cases of cold feet and legs, the patient should be made to sit with his feet and legs immersed up to the knees in as hot water as he can bear. A little mustard powder can be added to the water. The foot bath should not last for more than fifteen minutes. This treatment improves the local circulation and gives immediate relief.

In cases of common cold and sore throat a steam kettle which is very much like an ordinary tea kettle with a long nozzle can be used for applying steam to the nose or throat. A rubber tube of required length can be attached to any ordinary kettle for this purpose.

13

ETHER *(AKASH)*

Akash is a difficult word to translate as are indeed all the other four elements. For *pani* is not mere water in the original, nor *vayu* mere wind, or *prithvi* mere earth, or *teja* mere light. Perhaps the nearest equivalent is emptiness taken in its literal sense. And it is horribly inexpressive of the original. All the five in the original are as living as life. If, however, we take either as the nearest equivalent for *akash,* we must say that we know very little about ether itself and *akash* much less. Our knowledge of its therapeutic uses is still more limited. *Akash* might be taken for the empty space surrounding the earth and the atmosphere around it. On a clear day, on looking up, one sees a beautiful mauve blue canopy which is known the *akash* or sky. So far as we are concerned, this sky or the ether is limitless. We are surrounded by it on every side, and there is no nook or corner without it. Generally we imagine that the sky is something resting upon the high, it is the blue canopy above us. But the sky is as much above is as below and all around us. We move round and round with the earth. Therefore the *akash* is round and everybody is within it. It

> Akash might be taken for the empty space surrounding the earth and the atmosphere around it

is an envelope whose outermost surface is measureless. The lower strata of the *akash* for a number of miles are filled with air. But for this man would become suffocated in spite of the emptiness. True, we cannot see the air, but we can feel it when in motion. Take out air say from an empty bottle and create a vacuum, but who can pump out the vacuum itself? That is *akash*.

This *akash* we have to make use of to maintain or to regain health. Air being most essential to sustain life, nature has made it omnipresent. But the omnipresence of air is only relative. It is not limitless in reality. Scientists tell that after a certain number of miles above the earth there is no air. It is said that earthy creatures cannot exist outside this atmosphere. This statement may or may not be true. All that we are concerned with here is that *akash* extends beyond the atmosphere. Some day the scientists might prove that what we call ether is also something which fills the empty space *akash*. Then we will have to discover a new name for the empty space that holds neither air nor the ether. Be that as it may, the mystery of this empty space all around us is most intriguing. We cannot solve it unless we can solve the mystery of God Himself. This much might be said that the more we utilize this great element *akash* the healthier we will be. The first lesson to be learnt is this that we should not put any partitions between ourselves and the sky the infinite which is very near and yet very far away. If our bodies could be in contact with the sky without the intervention of houses, roofs and even clothes, we are likely to enjoy the maximum amount of health. This is not possible for everyone. But all can and should accept the validity of the statement and adapt life accordingly. To the extent that we are able to approach the state in practice, we will enjoy contentment and peace of mind. This train of thought taken to the extreme leads us to a condition when even the body becomes an obstacle separating man from the infinite. To understand this truth is to become indifferent to the dissolution of the body. For to lose oneself in the infinite is to find oneself. The body thus ceases to be a vehicle for self-indulgence. Man will make use of his body for the attempt and will discover that he is part of and one with all the life that surrounds him. This must mean service of mankind and through it finding God.

To return from the high flight, this train of thought will make the thinker keep his surrounding as open as possible. He will not fill the house with unnecessary furniture and will use the minimum of clothes that are necessary. Many households are so packed with all sorts of unnecessary decorations and furniture which one can very well do without; that a simple living man will feel suffocated in those surroundings. They are nothing but means of harbouring dust, bacteria and insects. Here in the house where I am under detention, I feel quite lost. The heavy furniture, chairs, tables, sofas, bedsteads, innumerable looking-glasses, all get on my nerves. The expensive carpets on the floors collect large amount of dust and act as a breeding place for insect life.

> He who will establish contact with the infinite possesses nothing and yet possesses everything

One day the carpet in one of the rooms was taken out for dusting. It was not one man's work. Six men spent the afternoon in doing the job. They must have removed at least ten pounds of dust. When the carpet was put back in its place it had a new feel about it. These carpets cannot be taken out and dusted everyday. Such treatment will wear out the carpets and greatly increase the expenditure of labour. But this is by way. What I mean to say is this that my desire to be in tune with the infinite has saved me from many complications in life. It led not merely to simplicity of household and dress but all round simplicity in the mode of my life. In a nutshell, and in the language of the subject under discussion, I have gone on creating more and more contact with *akash*. With the increase in the contact went improvement in health. I had more contentment and peace of mind and the desire for belongings almost disappeared. He who will establish contact with the infinite possesses nothing and yet possesses everything. In the ultimate analysis, man owns that of which he can make legitimate use and which he can assimilate. If everybody

Ether (Akash) **61**

followed this rule, there would be room enough for all and there would be neither want nor overcrowding.

It follows that one should make it a point to sleep in the open. Sufficient covering should be used to protect oneself against the inclemencies of the weather against cold and dew. In rainy season an umbrella like a roof without walls should be used for keeping the rain out. For the rest, the starlit blue canopy should form the roof so that whenever one opens one's eyes, he or she can feast them on the ever changing beautiful panorama of the heavens. He will never tire of the scene and it will not dazzle or hurt his eyes. On the contrary, it will have a soothing effect on him. To watch the different starry constellations floating in their majesty is a least for the eyes. One who establishes contact with the stars as living witnesses to all his thoughts will never allow any evil or impurity to enter his mind and will enjoy peaceful, refreshing sleep.

Let us descend from the *akash* above and immediately about us. Thus the skin has millions of pores. If we fill up the empty space within these pores, we will simply die. Any clogging in the pores therefore must interfere with the even flow of health. Similarly we must not fill up the digestive tract with unnecessary foodstuffs. We should eat only as much as we need and no more. Often one overeats or eats indigestible things without being aware of it. An occasional fast, say once a week or if one is unable to fast for the whole day, one should miss one meal during the day. Nature abhors a vacuum is only partially true. Nature constantly demands a vacuum. The vast space surrounding us is the standing testimony of the truth.

14

SUN

As in the case of the other elements, which have been already dealt with, man cannot do without sunlight. The sun is the source of light and heat. If there was no sun, there would be neither light nor warmth. Unfortunately we do not make full use of sunlight and consequently we are unable to enjoy perfect health. Sunbath is as useful as ordinary water bath though the two cannot replace one another. In cases of debility and slow circulation, exposure of the uncovered body to the morning sun acts as an all-round general tonic and accelerates the metabolism. The morning sun has the largest amount of ultra-violet rays which are a most effective component of the sun's rays. If the patient feels cold, he should lie in the sun covered up and gradually expose more and more of his body as he gets use to it. One can also take the sunbath pacing up and down in the sun without any clothes on, in a private enclosure or in other place away from public gaze. If such a place is not within easy reach, one can just cover up the private parts by tying up a piece of cloth or a *langoti* and expose the rest of his body to the sun.

> The morning sun has the largest amount of ultra-violet rays

I know many persons who have been benefited by sunbaths. It is a well-known treatment for tuberculosis. Sunbath or heliotherapy is no longer confined to the sphere of naturopathy. Orthodox medicine has taken it up from naturopathy and developed it further. In cold countries, special glass buildings have been constructed under medical supervision, so that the glass lets in the sun's rays and at the same time protects patients against the cold.

Sun treatment often results in the cure of intractable ulcers. To produce sweating I have made patients lie in the sun at about 11 a.m. , *i.e.* a little before midday. The experiment has been successful and the patients are soon bathed in sweat. In these cases the head should be protected from the sun by means of a cold mud poultice. Banana or any other leaves can keep the head cool and well-protected. The head should never be exposed to strong sunlight.

15

IMPORTANCE OF AIR

This fifth element is as important as the four already discussed in the foregoing pages. The human body which is composed of the five elements cannot do without any one of them. Therefore no one should be afraid of air. Generally, whenever our people go, they make devices to keep out the sun and the air and thus jeopardize their health. If one cultivates the habit of living in the open in the midst of plenty of fresh air, right from childhood, the body will become hardened and he or she will never suffer from cold in the head and the like ailments. I have said enough about the importance of fresh air in an earlier chapter. There is no occasion, therefore, to repeat here what has already been said.

SECTION III

The Moral Basis of Vegetarianism

❦ ❦ ❦

It is health that is real wealth and not pieces of gold and silver

16

FOOD VALUES

Whilst it is true that man cannot live without air and water, the thing that nourishes the body is food. Hence the saying, food is life.

Food can be divided into three categories: vegetarian, flesh, and mixed. Flesh foods include fowl and fish. Milk is an animal product and cannot by any means be included in a strictly vegetarian diet. It serves the purpose of meat to a very large extent. In medical language it is classified as animal food. A layman does not consider milk to be animal food. On the other hand, eggs are regarded by the layman as a flesh food. In reality, they are not. Nowadays sterile eggs are also produced. The hen is not allowed to see the cock and yet it lays eggs. A sterile egg never develops into a chick. Therefore, he who can take milk should have no objection to taking sterile eggs.

> Milk is an animal product and cannot by any means be included in a strictly vegetarian diet

Medical opinion is mostly in favour of a mixed diet, although there is a growing school, which is strongly of the opinion that anatomical and physiological evidence is in favour of man being a vegetarian. His teeth, his stomach, intestines, etc. seem to prove that nature has meant man to be a vegetarian.

Vegetarian diet, besides grains, pulses, edible roots, tubers and leaves, includes fruits, both fresh and dry. Dry fruits include nuts like almonds, pistachio, walnuts, etc.

17

UNFIRED FOOD

(In the course of a letter from Coonoor, dated 26-7-1929, addressed to Gandhiji in connection with his experiments in dietetics, Dr. R. McCarrison had written as follows:)

"One of the great faults in Indian diets at the present day is their deficiency in vitamin A, in suitable protein and in certain salts; and the greatest nutritional need of India is the freer use of good milk and its products which supply these factors. There can be no doubt in the minds of those of us who have devoted a life time to the study of nutrition that milk is one of the greatest blessings given to mankind.

> Milk is one of the greatest blessings given to mankind

And to one like myself, whose work is to learn the truth and spread it, the scarcity of this food in India and the lack of appreciation of its value are matters of grave concern. Do not, I beg of you, decry it; for a pint of milk a day will do more for young India than most things I thought of. It is, for example, to deficiency of vitamin A that we owe so much disease of the bowels and lungs, so much disease of the bladder (such as 'stone') and so much anaemia in this country.

I am glad you are taking interest in the matter of food and I agree with much that you say. But let me assure you that a little more 'fortissimo' on the 'milk and milk products' theme will do great good when you are leading the orchestra of Truth.

P. S. When next you make an Andhra tour, avoid "the extreme weakness", which overtook you in your last one, by taking a pint of milk a day!

(Commenting on Dr. McCarrison's letter Gandhiji wrote as under:)

I publish this letter thankfully and wish that other men versed in medical science would also guide me. In making the experiment, I am trying to find out the truth about food in so far as it is possible for a layman to do so.

As for Dr. McCarrison's argument about the necessity of animal food. I dare not as a layman combat it, but I may state that there are medical men who are decidedly of opinion that animal food including milk is not instinct and upbringing. I personally favour a purely vegetarian diet, and have for years been experimenting in finding a suitable vegetarian combination. But there is no danger of my decrying milk until I have obtained overwhelming evidence in support of milkless diet. It is one of many inconsistencies of my life that whilst I am in my own person avoiding milk, I am conducting a model dairy which is already producing cow's milk that can successfully compete with any such milk produced in India in purity and fat content.

Notwithstanding Dr. McCarrison's claim for medical science I submit that scientists have not yet explored the hidden possibilities of the innumerable seeds, leaves and fruits for giving the fullest possible nutrition to mankind. For one thing the tremendous vested interests that have grown round the belief in animal food prevent the medical profession from approaching the question with complete detachment. It almost seems to me that it is reserved for lay enthusiasts to cut their way through a mountain of difficulties even at the risk of their lives to find the truth. I should be satisfied if scientists would lend their assistance to such humble seekers.

As a searcher for Truth I deem it necessary to find the perfect food for a man to keep body, mind and soul in a sound condition. I believe that the search can only succeed with unfired food, and that in the limitless vegetable kingdom there is an effective substitute for milk, which every medical man admits, has its drawbacks and which is designed by nature not for man but for babies and young ones of lower animals. I should count no cost too dear for making a search which in my opinion is so necessary from more points of view than one. I therefore still seek information and guidance from kindred spirits.

> Inclusion of a small quantity of raw vegetables like cucumber, vegetable marrow, pumpkin, gourd, etc. in one's menu is more beneficial to health than the eating of large quantities of the same cooked

If one may take ripe fruit without cooking I see no reason why one may not take vegetables too in an uncooked state provided one can properly digest them. Dialecticians are of the opinion that the inclusion of a small quantity of raw vegetables like cucumber, vegetable marrow, pumpkin, gourd, etc. in one's menu is more beneficial to health than the eating of large quantities of the same cooked. But the digestions of most people are very often so impaired through a surfeit of cooked fare that one should not be surprised if at first they fail to do justice to raw greens, though I can say from personal experience that no harmful effect will follow if a *tola* or two of raw greens are taken with each meal provided one masticates them thoroughly. It is a well-established fact that one can derive a much greater amount of nourishment from the same quality of food if it is masticated well. The habit of proper mastication of food inculcated by the use of uncooked greens, therefore, if it does nothing else, will at least enable one to do with less quantity of food and thus not only make for economy in consumption but also automatically reduced the dietetic himsa that one commits to sustain life.

Therefore, whether regarded from the viewpoint of dietetics or that of *ahimsa*, the use of uncooked vegetables is not only free from all objections but is to be highly recommended. Of course, it goes without saying that if the vegetables are to be eaten raw extra care will have to be exercised to see that they are not stale, over-ripe or rotten, or otherwise dirty.

18

VEGETARIANISM

A correspondent is born in a meat-eating family. He has successfully resisted the pressure from his parents to return to the flesh-pot. "But", he says, "in a book I have before me, I read the opinion of swami Vivekanand on the subject and feel a good deal shaken in my belief. The Swami holds that for Indians in their present state flesh diet is a necessity and he advises his friends to eat flesh freely. He even goes so far as to say, "If you incur any sin thereby throw it upon me; I will bear it.' I am now in a fix whether to eat flesh or not."

This blind worship of authority is a sign of weakness of mind. If the correspondent has such a deep seated conviction that flesh eating is not right, why should he be moved by the opinion to the contrary of the whole world? One needs to be slow to form convictions, but once formed they must be defended against the heaviest odds.

> One needs to be slow to form convictions, but once formed they must be defended against the heaviest odds

As for the opinion of the great Swami, I have not seen actual writing but I fear the correspondent has correctly quoted him. My opinion is well known. I do not regard flesh-food as necessary for us at any stage and under any clime in which it is possible for human beings ordinarily to live. I hold flesh-food to be unsuited to our species. We err in copying the lower animal world if we are superior to it. Experience teaches that animal food is unsuited to those who would curb their passions.

But it is wrong to overestimate the importance of food in the formation of character or in subjugating the flesh. Diet is a powerful factor not to be neglected. But to sum up all religion in terms of diet, as is often done in India, is as wrong as it is to disregard all restraint in regard to diet and to give full reins to one's appetite. It is necessary, therefore, to correct the error that vegetarianism has made us weak in mind or body or passive or inert in action. The greatest Hindus have invariably been vegetarians. Who could show greater activity than say Shankara or Dayanand in their times?

But my correspondent must not accept me as his authority. The choice of one's diet is not a thing to be based on faith. It is a matter for everyone to reason out for himself. There has grown up especially in the West an amount of literature on vegetarianism which any seeker after truth may study with profit. Many eminent medical men have contributed to this literature. Here, in India, we have not needed any encouragement for vegetarianism. For it has been hitherto accepted as the most desirable and the most respectable thing.

One should not eat in order to please the palate but just to keep the body going. When each organ of sense serves the body and through the body the soul, its special relish disappears, and then alone does it begin to function in the way nature intended it to do.

Any number of experiments is too small and no sacrifice is too great for attaining this symphony with nature. But unfortunately the current is nowadays flowing strongly in the opposite direction. We are not ashamed to sacrifice a multitude of other lives in decorating the perishable body and trying to prolong its existence for a few fleeting moments with the result that we kill ourselves, we give rise to a hundred new ones; in trying to enjoy the pleasures of sense, we lose in the end even our capacity for enjoyment. All this is passing before our very eyes, but there are none so blind as those who will not see.

There is a great deal of truth in the saying that man becomes what he eats. The grosser the food the food the grosser the body.

I do feel that spiritual progress does demand at some stage that we should cease to kill our fellow creatures for the satisfaction of our bodily wants. The beautiful lines of Goldsmith occurs to me as I tell you of my vegetarian fad:

No flocks that range the valley free
To slaughter I condemn;
Taught by the Power that pities me
I learn to pity them

19

NOT AN END IN ITSELF

Abstemiousness from intoxicating drinks and drugs, and from all kinds of foods, especially meat, is undoubtedly a great aid to the evolution of the spirit, but it is by no means an end in itself. Many a man eating meat and with everybody living in the fear of God is nearer his freedom than a man religiously abstaining from meat and many other things, but blaspheming God in every one of his acts.

Abjure brinjals or potatoes by all means, if you will, but do not for heaven's sake begin to feel yourself self-righteous or flatter yourself that you are practising *ahimsa* on that account. The very idea is enough to make one blush. *Ahimsa* is not a mere matter of dietetics, it transcends it. What a man eats or drinks matters little; it is the self-denial, the self-restraint behind it that matters. By all means practise as much restraint in the choice of the articles of your diet as you like. The restraint is commendable, even necessary, but it touches wide latitude in the matter of diet and yet may be a personification of *ahimsa* and compel our homage, if his heart overflows with love and melts at another's woe, and has been purged of all passions. On the other hand, a man always over-scrupulous in diet is an utter stranger to *ahimsa* and a pitiful wretch, if he is a slave to selfishness and passions and is hard of heart.

I am painfully aware of the fact that my desire to continue life in the body involves me in constant *himsa*. That is why I am becoming growingly indifferent to this physical body of mine. For instance, I know that in the act of respiration I destroy innumerable invisible germs floating in the air. But I do not stop breathing. The consumption of vegetables involves *himsa*, but I find that I cannot give them up. Again, there is *himsa* in the use of antiseptics, yet I cannot bring myself to discard the use of disinfectants like kerosene, etc. to rid myself of the mosquito pest and the like. I suffer snakes to be killed in the Ashram when it is impossible to catch them and put them out of harm's way. I ever tolerate the use of the stick to drive the bullocks in the Ashram. Thus there is no end of *himsa* which I directly and indirectly commit. If, as a result of this humble confession of mine, friends choose to give me up as lost I would be sorry, but nothing will induce me to try to conceal my imperfection in the practice of *ahimsa*. All I claim for myself is that I am ceaselessly trying to understand the implications of great ideals like *ahimsa* and to practise them in thought, word and deed and that not without a certain measure of success as I think. But I know that I have long distance yet to cover in this direction.

20

THE MORAL BASIS OF VEGETARIANISM

(Address to the London Vegetarian Society* on 20th November, 1931.)

When I received the invitation to be present at this meeting, I need not tell you how pleased I was, because it revived old memories and recollections of pleasant friendships formed with vegetarians. I feel especially honoured to find on my right Mr. Henry Salt. It was Mr. Salt's book, *A Plea for Vegetarianism*, which showed me why, apart from a hereditary habit, and a part from my adherence to a vow administered to me by my mother, it was right to be a vegetarian. He showed me why it was a moral duty incumbent on vegetarians not to live upon fellow-animals. It is, therefore, a matter of additional pleasure to me that I find Mr. Salt in our midst.

I do not propose to take up your time by giving you my various experiences of vegetarianism, nor do I want to tell you something of the great difficulty that faced me in London itself in remaining staunch to vegetarianism, but I would like to share with you some of the thoughts that have developed in me in connection with vegetarianisms. Forty years ago I used to mix freely with vegetarians. There was that time hardly a vegetarian restaurant in London that I had not visited. I made it a point, out of curiosity, to visit every one of them. Naturally, therefore, I came into close contact with many vegetarians. I found at the tables, that largely the conversation turned upon food and disease. I also found that the vegetarians who were struggling to stick to their vegetarianism were finding it difficult from health point of view. I do not know whether, nowadays, you have those debates that were held between vegetarians and vegetarians, and between vegetarians and non-vegetarians. I remember one such debate, between Dr. Densmore, and the late Dr. T. R. Allinson. Then vegetarians had a habit of taking nothing but food and nothing but disease. I feel that is the worst way of going about the business. I notice also that it is those persons who become vegetarians because they are suffering form some disease or other that is from purely the health point of view. It is those persons who largely fall back. I discovered that for remaining staunch vegetarianism a man requires a moral basis.

For me that was a great discovery in my search after truth. At an early age in the course of my experiments, I found that a selfish basis would not serve the purpose of taking a man higher and higher along the paths of evolution. What was required was an altruistic purpose. I found also that health was by no means the monopoly of vegetarians. I found many people having no bias one way or the other, and that non-vegetarians were able to show, generally speaking, good health. I also found that several vegetarians found it impossible to remain vegetarians because they had made food a fetish and because they thought that by becoming vegetarians they could eat as much lentils, haricot beans, and cheese as they liked. Of course those people could not possibly keep their health. Observing along these lines, I saw that a man should eat sparingly and now and then fast. No man or woman really ate sparingly or consumed just that quantity which the body requires and no more. We easily fall a prey to the temptations of the palate, and therefore when thing taste delicious we do

> **A man should eat sparingly and now and then fast**

The Moral Basis of Vegetarianism

not mind taking a morsel or two more. But you cannot keep health under those circumstances. Therefore I discovered that in order to keep health, no matter what you ate, it was necessary to cut down the quantity of your food, and reduce the number of meals. Becomes moderate; err on the side of less, rather than on the side of more. When I invite friends to share their meals with me I never press them to take anything except only what they require. On the contrary, I tell them not to take a thing if they do not want to.

What I want to bring to your notice is that vegetarians need to be tolerant if they want to convert others to vegetarianism. Adopt a little humility. We should appeal to the moral sense of the people who do not see eye to eye with us. If a vegetarian became ill, and a doctor prescribed beef-tea, then I would not call him a vegetarian. A vegetarian is made of sterner stuff. Why? Because it is for the building of the spirit and not of the body. Man is more than meat. It is the spirit in man for which we are concerned. Therefore vegetarians should have that moral basis that a man was not born carnivorous animal, but born to live on the fruits and herbs that the earth grows. I know we must all err. I would give up milk if I could, but I cannot. I have made that experiment times without number I could not after a serious illness, regain my strength unless I went back to milk. That has been the tragedy of my life. But the basis of my vegetarianism is not physical, but moral. If anybody said that I should die if I did not take beef tea or mutton, even under medical advice, I would prefer death. That is the basis of my vegetarianism. I would love to think that all of us who called ourselves vegetarians should have that basis. There were thousands of meat-eaters who did not stay meat-eaters. There must be a definite reason for our making that change in our lives, for our adopting habits and customs different from society, even though sometimes that change may offend those nearest and dearest to us. Not for the world should you sacrifice a moral principle. Therefore the only basis for having a vegetarian

> Not for the world should you sacrifice a moral principle

society and proclaiming a vegetarian principle is, and must be, a moral one. I am not to tell you as I see and wander about the world, that vegetarian, on the whole, enjoy much better health than meat-eaters. I belong to a country which is predominantly vegetarian by habit or necessity. Therefore I cannot testify that shows much greater endurance, much greater courage, or much greater exemption from disease. Because it is a peculiar, personal thing. It requires obedience, and scrupulous obedience, to all the laws of hygiene.

Therefore, I think that what vegetarians should do is not to emphasize the physical consequences of vegetarianism, but to explore the moral consequences. While we have not yet forgotten that we share many things in common with the beast, we do not sufficiently realize that there are certain things which differentiate us from the beast. Of course, we have vegetarians in the cow and the bull which are better vegetarians than we are but there is something much higher which calls us to vegetarianism. Therefore, I thought that, during the few minutes which I give myself the privilege of addressing you. I would just emphasize the moral basis of vegetarianism. And I would say that I have found from my own experience, and the experience of thousands of friends and companions, that they find satisfaction, so far as vegetarianism is concerned, from the moral basis they have chosen for sustaining vegetarianism.

In conclusion, I think you all for coming here and allowing me to see vegetarians face to face. I cannot say I used to meet you forty or forty-two years ago. I suppose the faces of the London Vegetarian Society have changed. There are very few members who, like Mr. Salt, can claim association with the Society extending over forty years. Lastly, I would like you, if you want to ask me any questions, for I am a your disposal for a few minutes.

(Gandhiji was then asked to give his reasons for limiting his daily diet to five articles only, and he replied:)

That has no connection with vegetarianism. There was another reason. I had been a pampered child of nature. I had acquired then that notoriety that when I was invited to friends, they placed before me ample dishes of food. I told them I had come there to serve, and, personally, I should find myself dying by inches if I allowed myself to be pampered like that. So, in limiting myself to five ingredients of food, I served a double purpose. And I must finish all my eating before sundown. I have been saved many pitfalls by that. There are many discoveries about that in regard to health reasons. Dietists are saying that we are more and more tending towards simplifying diet, and that if one must live for health one must have one thing at a time and avoid harmful combination. I like the process of exclusion better than that of inclusion, because no two doctors have the same opinion.

> If one must live for health one must have one thing at a time and avoid harmful combination

Then, I think the restriction to five articles of food has helped me morally and materially. Materially because in a poor country like India it is not always possible to procure goat's milk, and it is a hard thing to produce fruit and grapes. Then, I go to visit poor people, and if I expected hot-house grapes, they would banish me. So, by restricting myself to five articles of food, it also serves the law of economy.

---

* During his student days in England Gandhiji had become a member of this society and had been elected subsequently as its Secretary. Dr. Oldfield was president, In 1931, when Gandhiji was in England for the Round Table Conference on India, he was invited to address the society.

21

OUR DAILY DIET

Rice

Whole, unpolished rice is unprocurable in the bazaars. It is beautiful to look at and rich and sweet to the taste. Mills can never compete with this unpolished rice. It is husked in a simple manner. Most of the paddy can be husked in a light *chakki* without difficulty. There are some varieties the husk of which is not separated by grinding. The best way of treating such paddy is to boil it first and then separate the chaff from the grain. This rice, it is said is most nutritious and , naturally, the cheapest. In the villages, if they husk their own paddy, it must always be cheaper for the peasants than the corresponding mill husked rice, whether polished or unpolished. The majority of rice found ordinarily in the *bazaars* is always more or less polished, whether hand-husked or mill husked. Wholly unpolished rice is always hand husked and is every time cheaper than the mill-husked rice, the variety being the same.

Wheat

The branless (wheat) flour is as bad as polished rice is the universal testimony of medical men. Whole wheat flour ground in one's *chakki* is any day superior and cheaper because the cost of grinding is saved. Again, in the whole wheat there is no loss of weight. In fine flour there is loss of wheat. The richest part of wheat is contained in its bran. There is a terrible loss of nutrition when the bran of wheat is removed. The villagers and others who eat whole wheat flour ground in their own *chakki* save their money and, what is more important their health. A large part of the millions that flour mills make will remain in and circulate among the deserving poor when village grinding is revived.

> There is a terrible loss of nutrition when the bran of wheat is removed

Cereals

Another physician quotes a text against the use of sprouted pulses but he too lacks actual experience for supporting his text. And this has been my complaint against many Ayurvedic physicians. I have no doubt that there is abundant ancient wisdom buried in the Sanskrit medical works. Our physicians appear to be too lazy to unearth that wisdom in the real sense of the term. They are satisfied with merely repeating the printed formula. Even as a layman I know many virtues are claimed for several Ayurvedic preparations. But where is their use, if they cannot be demonstrated today? I plead for the sake of this ancient science for a spirit of genuine search among our Ayurvedic physicians. I am as anxious as the tallest among them can be to free ourselves from the tyranny of Western medicines which are ruinously expensive.

Milk

It is my firm conviction that man need to take no milk at all, beyond the mother's milk that he takes as a baby. His diet should consist of nothing but sunbaked fruits and nuts. He can secure enough nourishment both for the tissues and the nerves from fruits like grapes and nuts like almonds. Restraint of the sexual and other passions becomes easy for a man who lives on such food. My co-workers and I have seen by experience that there is much truth in the Indian proverb that as a man eats, so shall he become.

Honey

My own experience of taking honey mixed with hot water extends to more than four years. I have experienced no ill-effect whatsoever. Objection has also been raised against it. But life is not governed by strict logic. It is an organic growth, seemingly irregular growth following its own law and logic. Western doctors bestow high praise upon it. Most of them who condemn the use of sugar in unmeasured terms speak highly of honey which they say does not irritate as refined sugar or even gur does.

Jaggery *(Gur)*

According to medical testimony *gur* is any day superior to refined sugar in food value, and if the villagers cease to make *gur* as they are beginning to do, they will be deprived of an important food adjunct for their children. They may do without *gur* themselves, but their children cannot without undermining their stamina. Retention of *gur* and its use by the people in general mean several crores of rupees retained by the villagers.

Fruits

No one perhaps, as far as I know, has eaten as much fruit as I have, having lived for six years on entirely fruits and nuts and always having a liberal supply of fruits as part of my ordinary diet. But I had in my mind, when writing, the special conditions of India. Its people should have, by reason of its extent and variety of climate, a most liberal supply of fruits, vegetables and milk. Yet it is the poorest country in this respect. I therefore suggested what seemed to me to be feasible. But I heartily endorse the proposition that for retaining health fresh fruits and fresh vegetables should form the main part of our diet. It is for the medical profession to study the peculiar condition of India and suggest the list of vegetables and fruits for local consumption. Wild berries, for instance, do not have sale value

> *For retaining health fresh fruits and fresh vegetables should form the main part of our diet*

but can be used for local consumption. This is a vast field for research. It can bring neither money nor perhaps fame. But it may earn the gratitude of the people.

I had introduced to me the leaves of sarsav, suwa, turnip-tops, carrot-tops, radish-tops and pea-nut leaves. Besides these, it is hardly necessary to state that the radish, turnip and carrot tubers are also known to be edible in their raw state. It is waste of money and 'good' taste, to cook these leaves or tubers. The vitamins contained in these vegetables are wholly or partially lost in cooking. I have called cooking these vegetables waste of 'good' taste because the uncooked vegetables have a natural good taste of their own which is destroyed by cooking.

22

MINIMUM DIET

Use one grain at a time. *Chapati*, rice and pulses, milk, *ghee*, *gur* and oil are used in ordinary households besides vegetables and fruit. I regard this as an unhealthy combination. Those who get animal protein in the shape of milk, cheese, eggs or meat need not use pulses at all. The poor people get only vegetable protein. If the well-to-do give up pulses and oils, they set free these two essentials for the poor who get neither animal protein nor animal fat. Then the grain eaten should not be sloppy. Half the quantity suffices when it is eaten dry and not sloppy. Half the quantity suffices when it is eaten with raw salads such as onion, carrot, radish, salad leaves, and tomatoes. An ounce or two of salads serve the purpose of eight ounces of cooked vegetables. *Chapatis* or bread should not be eaten with milk. To begin with, one meal may be raw vegetables and *chapati* or bread, and the other cooked vegetables with milk or curd.

> *Those who get animal protein in the shape of milk, cheese, eggs or meat need not use pulses at all*

Sweet dishes should be eliminated altogether. Instead *gur* in small quantities may be taken with milk or bread or by itself.

Fresh fruit is good to eat, but only a little is necessary to give tone to the system. It is an expensive article, and an over-indulgence by the well-to-do has deprived the poor and the ailing of an article which they need much more than the well-to-do.

Any medical man who has studied the science of dietetics will certify that what I have suggested can do no harm to the body, on the contrary it must conduce to better health.

❏ ❏ ❏